Harcourt Language

Reteach Activities Copying Masters

Grade 4

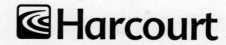

Orlando Boston Dallas Chicago San Diego

Visit *The Learning Site!*
www.harcourtschool.com

Copyright © by Harcourt, Inc.

All rights reserved. No part of this publication may be reproduced or transmitted in any form or by any means, electronic or mechanical, including photocopy, recording, or any information storage and retrieval system.

Teachers using HARCOURT LANGUAGE may photocopy complete pages in sufficient quantities for classroom use only and not for resale.

HARCOURT and the Harcourt Logo are trademarks of Harcourt, Inc.

Printed in the United States of America

ISBN 0-15-319113-9

5 6 7 8 9 10 073 2006 2005

Contents

Unit 1: Sentences

Declarative and Interrogative Sentences 1
Imperative and Exclamatory Sentences 2
Punctuating Four Kinds of Sentences 3
Complete and Simple Subjects 4
Nouns in Subjects 5
Combining Sentences: Compound Subjects 6
Complete and Simple Predicates 7
Verbs in Predicates 8
Combining Sentences: Compound Predicates 9
Sentences 10
Simple and Compound Sentences 11
Combining Sentences 12

Unit 2: More About Nouns and Verbs

Common and Proper Nouns 13
Singular and Plural Nouns 14
Abbreviations and Titles 15
Singular Possessive Nouns 16
Plural Possessive Nouns 17
Possessive Noun or Plural Noun? 18
Action Verbs 19
Linking Verbs 20
Using Forms of *Be* 21
Main Verbs and Helping Verbs 22
More About Main Verbs and Helping Verbs 23
Contractions with *Not* 24

Unit 3: More About Verbs

Verb Tenses 25
Present-Tense Verbs 26
Subject-Verb Agreement 27
Past-Tense Verbs 28
More About Past-Tense Verbs 29
Subject-Verb Agreement 30
Future-Tense Verbs 31
More About Future-Tense Verbs 32
Choosing the Correct Tense 33
Irregular Verbs 34
More Irregular Verbs 35
Commonly Misused Verbs 36

iii

Unit 4: Pronouns, Adjectives, and Adverbs

Pronouns and Pronoun Antecedents 37
Subject and Object Pronouns 38
Using *I* and *Me; We* and *Us* 39
Possessive Pronouns 40
Contractions with Pronouns 41
Homophones 42
Adjectives 43
Adverbs 44
Adjective or Adverb? 45
Other Kinds of Adverbs 46
Comparing with Adjectives and Adverbs 47
Special Forms 48

Unit 5: Phrases and Clauses

Prepositions 49
Object of the Preposition 50
Using Prepositional Phrases 51
Independent Clauses 52
Dependent Clauses 53
Distinguishing Independent and Dependent
    Clauses 54
Complex Sentences 55
More About Complex Sentences 56
Commas in Complex Sentences 57
Sentence Fragments 58
Run-on Sentences 59
Correcting Sentence Errors 60

Unit 6: Usage and Mechanics

Commas 61
Colons 62
Commas Versus Colons 63
Underlining and Using Quotation Marks
    in Titles 64
Capitalizing Words in Titles 65
Hyphens 66
Quotation Marks in Direct Quotations 67
Quotation Marks with Dialogue 68
Punctuating Dialogue 69
Easily Confused Words: Homophones 70
Negatives 71
Avoiding Double Negatives 72

Index 73–74

How to Use *Reteach Activities Copying Masters*

Students have different learning styles. The challenge for teachers is to help each student achieve success through activities that make use of his or her strength, whether **visual, auditory,** or **kinesthetic.**

The *Reteach Activities Copying Masters* provide alternative strategies for reinforcing the grammar concepts introduced in the *Pupil Edition.* For each grammar concept in **Harcourt Language,** three activities are provided—one for visual, one for auditory, and one for kinesthetic learners. The activities can be copied and cut apart for distribution to individuals or groups of students.

Identifying Learning Styles

The following description of these three modalities will help you identify the learning styles of individuals in your classroom and choose activities that will reach all learners. Keep in mind, however, that a student may benefit from activities in more than one modality. We learn and remember best when all our senses are engaged. You may need to try different kinds of activities with students who are having difficulty to find which ones are helpful.

Visual Learners

Visual learners learn best when they **see words, colors,** or **pictures.** When they can only listen, they translate what they hear into mental images. They respond well to demonstrations and to descriptions that allow them to create pictures in their minds. They can also be motivated through videos, diagrams, maps, charts, computer graphics, and opportunities for drawing and painting.

Look for

- interest in pictures and drawing
- attention to visual detail in the environment
- strong spatial awareness and sense of order
- sensitivity to the way words look
- preference for written information

Reteach Activities Copying Masters

Auditory Learners

Auditory learners learn best through listening and speaking. They often solve problems by **talking their way through the steps.** Ways to motivate these learners include opportunities for group work and discussion, oral storytelling, music, jingles, poetry, videos, audiotapes, and the use of tape recorders.

Look for

- preference for spoken information
- eagerness to answer questions orally
- good listening skills
- interest in group work and discussion
- tendency to think aloud

Kinesthetic Learners

Kinesthetic learners need to have abstract concepts made concrete. They learn best when some form of physical activity is involved. These students prefer manipulating concrete objects to looking at pictures or listening to explanations. They enjoy role play, creative movement, acting out stories and ideas, and hands-on activities.

Look for

- high energy level
- difficulty dealing with abstractions
- interest in touching and manipulating objects
- strong tactile sensitivity
- interest in painting, modeling, or building

Reteach Activities Copying Masters

Declarative and Interrogative Sentences

Read the sentences. Underline each declarative sentence. Draw a circle around each interrogative sentence.

<u>Missy wants to be an engineer.</u>

<u>Stan likes woodworking.</u>

(Does Joseph want to be a doctor?)

<u>Melanie wants to be a vet.</u>

<u>Hank wants to build houses.</u>

(Would you be a good salesperson?)

Visual

Declarative and Interrogative Sentences

What job would you like to have?

Tell a partner about a job you think you would enjoy. Use declarative sentences. Have your partner listen carefully and ask questions about the job. Then listen while your partner tells you about a job. Use interrogative sentences to find out more.

Auditory

Declarative and Interrogative Sentences

Think of a job you would enjoy.

Pantomime the job for a partner. Let your partner ask questions to find out what the job is. Answer the questions with declarative sentences. Take turns pantomiming and guessing.

Kinesthetic

Teacher: Cut apart the activities and distribute to students based on the modalities that are their strengths.
(Visual) Have students write their own declarative and interrogative sentences.
(Auditory) Ask a third student to observe to make sure each partner uses the correct type of sentence.
(Kinesthetic) Begin by brainstorming a list of jobs with students.

Reteach Activities • Sentences   Unit 1 • Chapter 1   1

Imperative and Exclamatory Sentences

Read the sentences. Underline each exclamatory sentence. Draw a circle around each imperative sentence.

<u>How exciting a class pet show will be!</u>

(Remember to bring in your pets.)

<u>How terrible I feel!</u>

(Please help me catch my iguana.)

Visual

Imperative and Exclamatory Sentences

With a partner, think of imperative sentences you might use to train a pet. Think of commands for different pets, such as cats, dogs, and birds. Practice saying the commands in a way that a pet would obey. Then think of exclamations that let the pet know what a good job it did. Say them in a way that would show a pet how pleased you are.

Auditory

Imperative and Exclamatory Sentences

Give a command to a partner about something you might do to take care of a pet, such as "Walk the dog now." Have your partner role play the command. Then use an exclamation to praise your partner, such as "Great job!" Take turns so that your partner can give commands and praise while you perform the commands.

Kinesthetic

Teacher: Cut apart the activities and distribute to students based on the modalities that are their strengths.
(Visual) Have volunteers copy the sentences on the board, using one color chalk for imperative sentences and another color for exclamatory sentences.
(Auditory) Have a third student record the commands in one list and the exclamations in another.
(Kinesthetic) Tell student actors to remain still if their partner's command is not in the form of an imperative sentence.

2 Unit 1 • Chapter 1   Reteach Activities • Sentences

Punctuating Four Kinds of Sentences

Decide whether the mark at the end of each sentence is correct. Cross out each mark that is incorrect. Write the correct mark in its place.

Ask your grandparents about the time before computers were invented!̶ .

What a change computers have made in our lives!

Computers make everything happen more quickly?̶ .

Have computers made our lives easier.̶ ?

Visual

Punctuating Four Kinds of Sentences

What would you do with a computer?

    Think about ways you use computers every day. Make up and say aloud to a partner sentences about computers. Use each of the four kinds of sentences at least once. After each sentence, have your partner tell which end punctuation mark should be used and why. Then switch roles.

Auditory

Punctuating Four Kinds of Sentences

Cut out the punctuation marks. Ask your partner to write a declarative, an interrogative, an imperative, and an exclamatory sentence about computers, leaving out the end punctuation mark. Place the correct punctuation mark at the end of each sentence. Then switch roles.

Kinesthetic

Teacher: Cut apart the activities and distribute to students based on the modalities that are their strengths.
(Visual) Ask students to explain their answers.
(Auditory) Use the sentences in the Visual activity as models.
(Kinesthetic) Extend the activity by having students place the punctuation cards face down in a pile, draw one, and make up an appropriate sentence.

Reteach Activities • Sentences   Unit 1 • Chapter 1   3

Complete and Simple Subjects

Read the paragraph. In each sentence, underline the complete subject and circle the simple subject.

The (students) in my class are too young to get jobs. My (friends) want to work anyway. (Volunteering) is the perfect solution. (One) of my friends reads with first graders. Another (friend) helps feed pets at a shelter. (I) want to find a volunteer job, too.

Visual

Complete and Simple Subjects

Think of a simple subject. Have your partner add words about the simple subject to make a longer, complete subject. Work together to finish the sentence. Repeat the finished sentence and name the simple subject and the complete subject. Then switch roles.

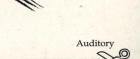

Auditory

Complete and Simple Subjects

Make up sentences with three friends. Write a simple subject at the top of a sheet of paper. Below that, the next person writes the simple subject and adds words to make a longer, complete subject. Have the third person add a predicate to make a complete sentence. Then fold the paper so that only the final sentence shows. Ask the fourth person to name the simple subject and the complete subject. Let a different person begin the next sentence.

Kinesthetic

Teacher: Cut apart the activities and distribute to students based on the modalities that are their strengths.
(Visual) You may want to write the paragraph on the board.
(Auditory) Students in a small group may think of other sentences for each simple subject.
(Kinesthetic) Have one student record all the simple and complete subjects.

Nouns in Subjects

Read each complete subject. Underline all the nouns. Circle the noun that is the simple subject.

The (newspaper) from our class

Every (student) in the class

The best (stories) in the paper

The (cartoons) on the last page

Visual

Nouns in Subjects

Say the sentence below aloud. With a partner, complete the sentence in as many different ways as you can by using different nouns to replace the word *blank*. Tell which noun is the simple subject of each sentence.

> The blank in the blank work on the school newspaper.

Auditory

Nouns in Subjects

Work with two or three other students. Make up a group sentence, with each student contributing one word at a time. Work together to include a noun as the simple subject. Write several sentences, changing the noun in each one.

Kinesthetic

Teacher: Cut apart the activities and distribute to students based on the modalities that are their strengths.
(Visual) Students can complete each sentence and underline any nouns they use in the predicates.
(Auditory) Have one student record the nouns used and count the number of different sentences.
(Kinesthetic) After each sentence, have students who named nouns record the nouns they used.

Reteach Activities • Subjects/Nouns

Combining Sentences: Compound Subjects

Read each sentence. Circle the subject. Combine the sentences using a compound subject.

My (mother) will help.   (Mary) will help.
My mother and Mary will help.
_____

(Greg) hid the ball.   (Tisha) hid the ball.   (Alan) hid the ball.
Greg, Tisha, and Alan hid the ball.
_____

Visual

- -

Combining Sentences: Compound Subjects

Read aloud the pairs of sentences below. Ask a partner to combine them and name the nouns in the compound subject. Work together to make up new sentences to combine.

> Jamal picked up litter. Laura picked up litter.
>
> Andy will paint the fence. Mei will paint the fence.

Auditory

- -

Combining Sentences: Compound Subjects

With a partner, pantomime a job you could do together to help your community. Other group members can guess what the job is and make up sentences describing what you and your partner are doing. Work as a group to combine the sentences to make a compound subject.

Kinesthetic

- -

Teacher: Cut apart the activities and distribute to students based on the modalities that are their strengths.
(Visual) Have students turn over their papers and recall the original sentences.
(Auditory) Ask a volunteer to write the original sentences on the board and underline the parts that are the same.
(Kinesthetic) Have students name the nouns in the compound subject.

Reteach Activities • Subjects/Nouns

Complete and Simple Predicates

Read the paragraph. In each sentence, underline the complete predicate and circle the simple predicate.

Bobbie (saw) a toy on television. It (was) a popular toy. Bobbie (wanted) the toy badly. She (saved) her money for a month. She (thought) the toy was boring by then. She (put) her money in the bank instead.

Visual

Complete and Simple Predicates

What is a good way to save money?

Say a complete sentence about saving money for a toy. Have your partner repeat the whole sentence and name the simple predicate. Take turns making up sentences and naming the simple predicates.

Auditory

Complete and Simple Predicates

Take the role of a salesperson, and pretend to sell something to a partner.

Make up one sentence that tells a good reason for buying the object. Your partner can "buy" what you are selling by naming the complete predicate and the simple predicate.

Kinesthetic

Teacher: Cut apart the activities and distribute to students based on the modalities that are their strengths.
(Visual) Have students write about something they wish they hadn't spent money on and then underline complete predicates and circle simple ones.
(Auditory) Suggest that students begin by brainstorming words about how to save money.
(Kinesthetic) Students may enjoy using classroom objects as props.

Reteach Activities • Predicates/Verbs   Unit 1 • Chapter 4   7

Verbs in Predicates

Read each sentence. Circle the verb. Then underline the complete predicate.

Rudy (travels) all over the country.

He (enjoys) tall mountains.

He (enjoys) the hot, sunny deserts.

His favorite place (is) the ocean.

Visual

Verbs in Predicates

What would tourists see in your area?

With a partner, make up a commercial to encourage tourists to visit your area. Take turns making up sentences. After each sentence, name the verb and the complete predicate.

Auditory

Verbs in Predicates

Where would you like to take a vacation?

Write the word *verb* in large letters on an index card. Say sentences about vacations. Have your partner hold up the *verb* card whenever you use a verb. When you finish telling about a vacation you had, let your partner tell about a different vacation while you hold up the card to signal each verb.

Kinesthetic

Teacher: Cut apart the activities and distribute to students based on the modalities that are their strengths.
(Visual) Have students write new sentences on the board, leaving a blank for a partner to fill in the simple predicate.
(Auditory) Have students begin by listing interesting things about your area.
(Kinesthetic) Review action and linking verbs with students.

8   Unit 1 • Chapter 4   Reteach Activities   •   Predicates/Verbs

Combining Sentences: Compound Predicates

Read each sentence. Underline the simple predicate. Then use a conjunction and a compound predicate to combine the sentences. Circle the conjunction you use.

Salespeople <u>help</u> customers. Salespeople <u>take</u> orders. Salespeople <u>handle</u> complaints.

<u>Salespeople help customers, take orders, (and) handle complaints.</u>

Visual

- -

Combining Sentences: Compound Predicates

How do you do that job?

With a partner, choose a job you know. Think of all the things a person with that job does. Work together to make up a long sentence about the job. Use a compound predicate, and remember to use a conjunction.

Auditory

- -

Combining Sentences: Compound Predicates

Stand in a line with two or three other students.

One student should pantomime three actions. Make up a sentence with a compound predicate that tells what he or she did. Repeat the activity with each student.

Kinesthetic

- -

Teacher: Cut apart the activities and distribute to students based on the modalities that are their strengths.
(Visual) Remind students that the most common conjunctions are *and* and *or*.
(Auditory) Have students count the verbs in their longest sentence.
(Kinesthetic) Remind students to insert a conjunction before naming the last action.

Reteach Activities • Predicates/Verbs   Unit 1 • Chapter 4   9

Sentences

Read the paragraph. Underline each incomplete sentence. Then write a complete sentence to replace it.

   My favorite holiday is Thanksgiving. <u>Have different holiday traditions.</u> People celebrate in different ways. <u>In our family.</u>

Many people have different holiday traditions.

In our family we all cook dinner together.

Visual

Sentences

What is your favorite tradition?

   Say to a partner an incomplete sentence about something you do on a holiday. Ask your partner to tell what part is missing and complete the sentence. Then switch roles. Listen to what your partner likes to do. Repeat the completed sentences aloud together.

Auditory

Sentences

Have each member of your small group write on a sentence strip a sentence about a special holiday or celebration. Cut each sentence apart between the subject and predicate. Mix up everyone's sentence parts. Then match subjects with predicates to make complete sentences.

Kinesthetic

Teacher: Cut apart the activities and distribute to students based on the modalities that are their strengths.
(Visual) Ask students to add one more complete sentence to the paragraph.
(Auditory) Let students write their sentences on the board, erase the subject or predicate, and complete each sentence in a different way.
(Kinesthetic) As an alternative, each student can hold up one sentence part while other group members find the part that completes the sentence.

10   Unit 1 • Chapter 5   Reteach Activities • Simple and Compound Sentences

Simple and Compound Sentences

Read each sentence. Circle each simple sentence. Underline each compound sentence.

(My aunt lives in a suburb but works in the city.)

She likes the city, and she likes the country, too.

The country is peaceful, but the city is exciting.

Do you prefer the city, or do you like the country?

Simple and Compound Sentences

Do you have a favorite city?

With a partner, think of two facts about a city you have been to often. Use the facts to make up a compound sentence. Then use the same facts to make up a simple sentence with a compound predicate.

Simple and Compound Sentences

Cut simple and compound sentences from old magazines or newspapers. Glue the sentences on construction paper. With a partner, decide whether each sentence is simple or compound. Point to the simple and complete subjects and predicates in the sentences.

Teacher: Cut apart the activities and distribute to students based on the modalities that are their strengths.
(Visual) Have students explain the reasons for their answers.
(Auditory) Have students write down their sentences and point out the differences between the two.
(Kinesthetic) You may want to make this a small-group activity.

Reteach Activities • Simple and Compound Sentences   Unit 1 • Chapter 5   11

Combining Sentences

Read the sentences. Underline each compound sentence and circle the conjunction.

Kerry and Richard visited Mexico.

Richard went to the beach,(and) Kerry went to the museum.

The water was warm,(but) the waves were big.

The weather was cloudy but warm.

Richard jumped into a wave,(and) it knocked him down.

Visual

Combining Sentences

What do you know about your culture?

    Talk with a partner about your cultural heritage. Make up a compound sentence that tells something about your cultural history. Have your partner name the subjects and predicates.

Auditory

Combining Sentences

Think about your cultural heritage.

    Write *and, but, or,* and a comma on four index cards. Write two simple sentences about your cultural history on sentence strips. Ask your partner to use one of the conjunction cards and the comma card to turn the two simple sentences into one compound sentence. You may also need to change one of the capital letters.

Kinesthetic

Teacher: Cut apart the activities and distribute to students based on the modalities that are their strengths.
(Visual) Have a volunteer explain how to choose a conjunction and where to place a comma.
(Auditory) Suggest that students talk to family members to find out more about their cultural history.
(Kinesthetic) Remind students to change the capital letter on the second sentence, unless the sentence begins with *I* or a proper noun.

12 Unit 1 • Chapter 5   Reteach Activities • Simple and Compound Sentences

Common and Proper Nouns

Read the paragraph. Underline each common noun. Circle each proper noun.

(Rico) and I go to the same doctor. (Dr. Brown) gives us the same advice. She says to eat healthful foods and get some exercise. I take my dog, (Charlie), for walks, and (Rico) brings (Elmo). We go to (Stonecreek Park).

Visual

Common and Proper Nouns

Work with two or three partners.

Take turns reading aloud from a health or science book as the other group members listen. When the listeners hear a proper noun, they should stand to signal that the noun should begin with a capital letter.

Auditory

Common and Proper Nouns

Work with two or three students.

Each one should write two common nouns and two proper nouns on separate index cards. Place all the cards in a paper bag, and pass the bag from one person to another. The student with the bag takes out one card and reads it aloud. The other students tell whether the noun is common or proper.

Kinesthetic

Teacher: Cut apart the activities and distribute to students based on the modalities that are their strengths.
(Visual) Have students tell whether each noun is a person, place, thing, or idea.
(Auditory) Help students select a book or a chapter that includes many proper nouns.
(Kinesthetic) If necessary, let students use the *Pupil Edition* to locate common and proper nouns to write.

Reteach Activities • More About Nouns   Unit 2 • Chapter 7   13

Singular and Plural Nouns

Read each word pair. Circle each singular noun. Put a check mark next to each plural noun.

| children ✓ | tooth | body | stories ✓ | doctors ✓ |
| child | teeth ✓ | bodies ✓ | story | doctor |

| dozen | woman | knee | feet ✓ | box |
| dozens ✓ | women ✓ | knees ✓ | foot | boxes ✓ |

Visual

Singular and Plural Nouns

Sit in a circle with a group of friends. Take turns reading aloud a story everyone knows. When you hear a plural noun, raise your hand and spell it aloud. If you spell it correctly, it is your turn to read.

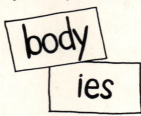

Auditory

Singular and Plural Nouns

Write *s*, *es*, and *ies* on separate index cards.

   Have a partner write a singular noun. Choose the card that will make the noun plural, and put it in the correct place. Trace over the letters in the plural noun with your finger. Take turns thinking of nouns. If a noun has an irregular plural, write the plural.

Kinesthetic

Teacher: Cut apart the activities and distribute to students based on the modalities that are their strengths.
(Visual) Have students explain the process for making each noun plural.
(Auditory) If students spell incorrectly, have them repeat the correct spelling after you.
(Kinesthetic) For each word, have students explain why they chose a particular ending.

Abbreviations and Titles

Read each sentence. Circle the word in the sentence that can be abbreviated. Write the abbreviations.

Ben has a dental appointment on (Tuesday).   Tues.

He'll take the bus to (Doctor) Winter's office.   Dr.

The bus goes up Lorain (Avenue).   Ave.

Ben's next appointment is in (September).   Sept.

Visual

Abbreviations and Titles

Do you know many abbreviations?

Read to a partner a word from the Common Abbreviations chart on page 96 in the *Pupil Edition*. Have your partner spell the abbreviation for the word you read. Make sure your partner adds a period. Take turns reading words and spelling abbreviations.

Auditory

Abbreviations and Titles

Write on index cards words from the Common Abbreviations chart on page 96 in the *Pupil Edition*. Have your partner write the abbreviations on other cards. Mix up the cards. Spread them out face down on a desk top. Then take turns turning up two cards and trying to match a word with its abbreviation.

Kinesthetic

Teacher: Cut apart the activities and distribute to students based on the modalities that are their strengths.
(Visual) After students finish, have them cover the sentences with their hand and tell the word for each abbreviation.
(Auditory) Students may write the abbreviations as they spell them aloud. They can use their list of abbreviations for review.
(Kinesthetic) Students can also use their cards for review.

Reteach Activities • More About Nouns   Unit 2 • Chapter 7

Singular Possessive Nouns

Draw a line from each sentence to the phrase with the matching possessive noun.

The markings of an animal can help it stay safe.   a rabbit's fur

A fawn blends in with the shadows of the forest.   an animal's markings

The fur of a rabbit may turn white in snow.   a fox's eyes

The white fur hides it from the eyes of a fox.   the forest's shadows

Visual

Singular Possessive Nouns

Have you ever seen a wild animal?

Tell a partner a fact about a wild animal. Use a singular possessive noun in your sentence. Ask your partner to listen for the possessive noun and then write it, using 's to show possession. Take turns telling facts and listening for singular possessive nouns.

Auditory

Singular Possessive Nouns

Think of the names of wild animals.

Write 's on an index card. Write the names of the animals on other cards. Choose an animal card and turn it into a singular possessive noun by placing the 's card at the end. Make up a sentence that includes the singular possessive noun.

Kinesthetic

Teacher: Cut apart the activities and distribute to students based on the modalities that are their strengths.
(Visual) Have students illustrate one of the sentences.
(Auditory) Let students display their sentences on an animal facts bulletin board.
(Kinesthetic) After students combine the cards, have them write the singular possessive form of the noun.

Plural Possessive Nouns

Read the paragraph. Underline each plural possessive noun. Draw an arrow to the word that tells what is owned.

The robins' nest is in that tree. There are four babies in the nest. The babies' beaks are always open. The parents bring food to fill the little birds' stomachs. We are lucky to have the robins. These birds are one of people's favorites.

Visual

Plural Possessive Nouns

Finish the phrase *of the* _____ with a plural noun. Use some plural nouns that end in *s* and some irregular plural nouns that do not end in *s*. Have your partner repeat the phrase and change the noun to the plural possessive form. Then write each plural possessive noun in the chart.

Add 's	Add an '

Auditory

Plural Possessive Nouns

Choose a partner. Write plural nouns on separate index cards. Include irregular plural nouns that do not end in *s*, too. Write an apostrophe on another card and 's on another card. Take turns choosing a noun card and adding one of the other cards to form a plural possessive noun.

Kinesthetic

Teacher: Cut apart the activities and distribute to students based on the modalities that are their strengths.
(Visual) Have students explain why the plural possessive form *people's* is different from the others.
(Auditory) Students may need to look at the *Pupil Edition* to recall nouns with irregular plurals.
(Kinesthetic) Ask a third student to check and record the plural possessive nouns in a chart like the one in the Auditory activity.

Reteach Activities • Possessive Nouns

Possessive Noun or Plural Noun?

Read each word pair. Circle each possessive noun. Write whether it is singular or plural.

(whale's) whale — singular

women (women's) — plural

(sharks') sharks — plural

(calves') calves — plural

Visual

Possessive Noun or Plural Noun?

Cut out these cards, and place your cards and your partner's cards face down in a pile. Take turns drawing a card and making up a sentence with a subject that has the kind of noun on the card. Have your partner listen and tell what kind of noun you used.

| singular possessive | plural possessive | plural, not possessive |

Auditory

Possessive Noun or Plural Noun?

Cut out these cards. On separate index cards, write four examples of each kind of noun. Mix up the noun cards and place them face down in rows. With a partner, take turns choosing a noun card. If you can correctly match the noun card with the card that tells what kind of noun it is, you can keep the noun card. Continue until all the noun cards are gone.

| singular possessive | plural possessive | plural, not possessive |

Kinesthetic

Teacher: Cut apart the activities and distribute to students based on the modalities that are their strengths.
(Visual) Have students write sentences, using one form of each noun.
(Auditory) If the partner cannot give the correct noun form, have students write the sentence and work together to get the right answer.
(Kinesthetic) As an alternative, have students sort the noun cards into categories based on word structure.

Action Verbs

Read the paragraph. Underline each action verb. Draw a circle around the subject it tells about.

In A.D. 79, a (volcano) destroyed the Roman city of Pompeii. (Ash) buried the city. (It) also preserved the city. Years later, (scientists) found the city's remains. The (remains) taught the world about life in ancient times.

- Visual ✂

Action Verbs

What do you know about volcanoes?

Find an article about a volcano in an encyclopedia, a magazine, a science book, or a social studies book. Read one paragraph aloud. Have your partner listen for action verbs and snap his or her fingers each time you read one. Pass the book to your partner and switch roles.

- Auditory

Action Verbs

Suppose that you live near a volcano.

Role play something you would do if you learned that the volcano was about to explode. Have your partner make up a sentence about what you are doing and name the action verb. Then switch roles and guess the action your partner is performing.

- Kinesthetic

Teacher: Cut apart the activities and distribute to students based on the modalities that are their strengths.
(Visual) Review with students that they have underlined the simple predicate and circled the simple subject.
(Auditory) You may wish to save time by providing articles for students to use.
(Kinesthetic) Have students record the action verbs they use.

Reteach Activities • Action Verbs and Linking Verbs   Unit 2 • Chapter 10   19

Linking Verbs

Read each sentence. Underline the linking verb. Circle the word that the linking verb connects to the subject.

The weather is (different) after a volcano erupts.

After an eruption, the sky grows (cloudy).

The air tastes (dusty).

The sun seems (dimmer).

Visual

Linking Verbs

Suppose that a cloud of volcanic ash has covered the sky. Role-play a conversation with a partner about how the large cloud of ash between you and the sun has changed your weather. Whenever one of you hears a linking verb, raise your hand.

Auditory

Linking Verbs

On separate index cards, write five nouns to use as subjects, five linking verbs, and five words that rename or describe the subjects.

Separate the cards into three piles—nouns, verbs, and other. Then, with a partner, take turns drawing a card from each pile. Use all three words in a sentence. Some sentences may be silly.

Kinesthetic

Teacher: Cut apart the activities and distribute to students based on the modalities that are their strengths.
(Visual) Have students name other linking verbs that could fit in each sentence.
(Auditory) Students may begin by brainstorming weather words.
(Kinesthetic) Have students mix all the cards together and take turns choosing one and identifying it as a noun, verb, or other.

20   Unit 2 • Chapter 10   Reteach Activities • Action Verbs and Linking Verbs

Using Forms of Be

Circle each sentence that has the correct form of *be*. If a form is incorrect, cross it out and write the correct form above it.

Natural disasters ~~is~~ *are* unlikely to happen to you.

(It is always good to be prepared, though.)

(Be sure to keep flashlights and water handy.)

A battery-powered radio ~~are~~ *is* helpful, too.

I ~~be~~ *am* sure you'll feel safer with a family safety kit.

Visual

Using Forms of Be

Sit across from a partner and say a subject.

Have your partner say the form of *be* that agrees with the subject. Take turns naming subjects and verbs. Start out slowly. Then speed up. See how quickly you and your partner can respond with the correct verb.

Auditory

Using Forms of Be

Write all the forms of *be* on separate index cards.

Sit in a circle with two or three students with the cards laid out face up in front of you. Have a group leader say a subject. Hold up the card with the form of *be* that agrees with the subject. Take turns being the leader.

Kinesthetic

Teacher: Cut apart the activities and distribute to students based on the modalities that are their strengths.
(Visual) Have students identify the subjects and make sure the subjects and verbs agree.
(Auditory) As an alternative, have the responding students say a predicate that begins with the correct linking verb.
(Kinesthetic) If students' responses are not the same, the group leader should resolve the problem.

Reteach Activities • Action Verbs and Linking Verbs

Main Verbs and Helping Verbs

Read each sentence. Underline the main verb. Circle the helping verb.

I (have) visited the seashore many times.

I (can) swim in the ocean on warm days.

I (will) go again next weekend.

(Do) you like the ocean too?

(Would) you come along with me?

Visual

Main Verbs and Helping Verbs

With a partner, take turns reading aloud from a book or an article about oceans. While your partner is reading, listen for helping verbs. Raise your hand each time you hear one. Keep a list of all the helping verbs you and your partner find.

Auditory

Main Verbs and Helping Verbs

Write a progressive sentence about the ocean with a small group of classmates.

The first person begins the sentence by writing one word and then passes the paper to the next person, who writes the next word, and so on. Be sure to use a helping verb in each sentence. When you finish one sentence, begin a new one. Reread the sentences and point to the helping verbs.

Kinesthetic

Teacher: Cut apart the activities and distribute to students based on the modalities that are their strengths.
(Visual) Have students write their own sentences about things they would do if they could visit the ocean.
(Auditory) After students write down helping verbs, have them mark which are forms of *be* and must agree with the subject.
(Kinesthetic) Have students use a highlighter to mark the helping verbs.

22 Unit 2 • Chapter 11   Reteach Activities • Main Verbs and Helping Verbs

More About Main Verbs and Helping Verbs

Read each sentence. Underline the main verb twice. Underline the helping verb once. Circle the word that comes between the two parts of the verb.

I have (often) watched the polar bears at the zoo.

In the summer, they are (always) resting in the cool water.

They do (not) sleep as much in the winter.

In the winter, they are (usually) playing.

Visual

- -

More About Main Verbs and Helping Verbs

What is a cold-weather animal?

   Say a sentence about a cold-weather animal to a partner. Use a helping verb and a main verb in your sentence. Ask your partner to repeat the sentence and to add an appropriate word between the helping verb and the main verb. Say two more sentences. Then switch roles so that your partner makes up three sentences.

Auditory

- -

More About Main Verbs and Helping Verbs

On sentence strips, write sentences about animals that live in cold climates. Use a helping verb and a main verb in each sentence. Cut apart each sentence strip between the main verb and the helping verb. Write on an index card a word that can come between the main verb and helping verb, and place it in the sentence.

| Penguins are | always | sliding on the ice. |

Kinesthetic

- -

Teacher: Cut apart the activities and distribute to students based on the modalities that are their strengths.
(Visual) Tell students to cover the extra word with a finger, read the sentence, and explain whether or not the sentence has the same meaning.
(Auditory) Students may begin by using the *Pupil Edition* to make a list of words that can come between main verbs and helping verbs.
(Kinesthetic) Have students tell how the extra word changes or improves the sentence.

Reteach Activities • Main Verbs and Helping Verbs

Contractions with *Not*

Circle the contraction in each sentence. Then draw a line to match the contraction to the correct words.

Earthquakes (aren't) any fun. ——————— have not

You (don't) want to be in one. ——————— are not

You (won't) know until it happens. ———— do not

You (haven't) any time to prepare. ———— will not

Visual

Contractions with *Not*

Would you like to be a fish?

Tell a partner about whether you think it would be fun to be a fish. Use as many contractions with *not* as you can. Have your partner stop you after every contraction with *not* and tell what two words make up the contraction. Then let your partner talk as you listen.

Auditory

Contractions with *Not*

With a partner, write the following phrases and contractions on separate index cards: *is not, isn't, were not, weren't, has not, hasn't, could not, couldn't, does not, doesn't, will not, won't, are not, aren't, was not, wasn't, should not, shouldn't, do not, don't.* Mix the cards up, and turn them face down in rows. Take turns picking up two cards at a time. Try to match each phrase with its contraction. Use the contraction in a sentence. Then let your partner take a turn.

Kinesthetic

Teacher: Cut apart the activities and distribute to students based on the modalities that are their strengths.
(Visual) Have students cover the original sentences and name the contraction for each group of words.
(Auditory) Have students list contraction sentences on a two-column chart with the headings *Fun* and *Not Fun*.
(Kinesthetic) Have students write their contraction sentences and trace over each contraction with a crayon or marker.

Verb Tenses

Circle the verb in each sentence. Then write the tense of the verb: *past*, *present*, or *future*.

Early artists (painted) on the walls of caves.   *past*

Today we (call) wall paintings murals.   *present*

Some modern artists (create) murals along freeways.   *present*

Someday we (will talk) about their designs.   *future*

Visual

Verb Tenses

Are you an artist?

   Tell a partner what kinds of art you did when you were a young child, what art you do now, and what artwork you think you will do when you get older. Pause after each sentence to let your partner name the tense of the verb in the sentence. Then exchange roles with your partner.

Auditory

Verb Tenses

What art projects do you like to do?

   Write *Present*, *Past*, and *Future* on separate index cards, and place the cards in a box. With a partner, take turns drawing a card from the box. Show the card to your partner, and make up a sentence about art using the verb tense you chose.

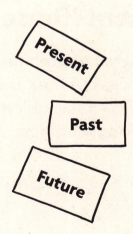

Kinesthetic

Teacher: Cut apart the activities and distribute to students based on the modalities that are their strengths.
(Visual) Have students explain their choices.
(Auditory) Ask a third student to observe to make sure each partner identifies the verb tense correctly.
(Kinesthetic) Students might also hold up the cards to identify the verb tense in sentences on classroom bulletin boards or posters.

Reteach Activities • Present-Tense Verbs   Unit 3 • Chapter 13

Present-Tense Verbs

Proofread the paragraph below. Cross out verbs that are spelled incorrectly. Write the correct spelling above the verb you crossed out.

Mom drops Shanti off at the art museum. Shanti ~~hurrys~~ *hurries* off to meet her friends. The girls rush inside. Shanti accidentally ~~brushs~~ *brushes* against a sculpture. "I'll have to be more careful," she ~~saies~~ *says*. The girls ~~looks~~ *look* at many different kinds of art. Shanti ~~feel~~ *feels* sad when it is time to go home.

Visual

- -

Present-Tense Verbs

Write *s*, *es*, and *ies* on index cards. Say a sentence that has a present-tense verb. Have your partner name the verb and hold up the card that shows the correct ending of the present-tense verb. If the verb does not end with *s*, *es*, or *ies*, your partner should sit still. Take turns making up sentences and holding up cards.

Auditory

- -

Present-Tense Verbs

Make a set of alphabet cards. Have your partner spell a verb with the cards. Cut out the cards below, and use them to show how the verb would be spelled if its subject were a singular noun. Take turns forming words and adding endings.

s	es	ies

Kinesthetic

Teacher: Cut apart the activities and distribute to students based on the modalities that are their strengths.
(Visual) Have students exchange papers to check each other's corrections.
(Auditory) Students can write the verb on the board and place the card beside or over it to show the correct spelling.
(Kinesthetic) If commercial alphabet cards are available, save time by distributing them to students.

26 Unit 3 • Chapter 13   Reteach Activities • Present-Tense Verbs

Subject-Verb Agreement

Circle the verb in each sentence. Then draw an arrow from the verb to the simple subject of the sentence.

Caleb (likes) all kinds of art.

He (enjoys) modern paintings.

Bright colors (make) him happy.

He (watches) mobiles in the breeze.

Visual

Subject-Verb Agreement

Read aloud a sentence with a present-tense verb from a book about art.

Pause to let your partner name the simple subject and the verb, and tell whether the subject and verb are singular or plural. Have your partner read another sentence while you listen and respond.

Auditory

Subject-Verb Agreement

In a small group, take turns pantomiming things an artist does while working. Have some group members perform alone, and have others perform with a partner. Viewers can guess what the actors are doing by making up a sentence about it. Remember to use a singular subject and verb for sentences about one student actor, and a plural subject and verb for sentences about more than one student actor.

Kinesthetic

Teacher: Cut apart the activities and distribute to students based on the modalities that are their strengths.
(Visual) Ask students to explain their answers.
(Auditory) Encourage students to select a book for young children, which is less likely to have long compound and complex sentences.
(Kinesthetic) Tell students to use action verbs without helping verbs in their sentences.

Reteach Activities • Present-Tense Verbs

Past-Tense Verbs

Above each underlined verb, write the verb in the past tense.

Most famous authors <u>start</u> *(started)* out just like you. They <u>borrow</u> *(borrowed)* books from the library. Soon they <u>decide</u> *(decided)* to write a book. At first, writing <u>seems</u> *(seemed)* hard. The new writers <u>toss</u> *(tossed)* away some of their writing. They <u>work</u> *(worked)* on anyway. Then, they <u>sell</u> *(sold)* their books to a publisher.

Visual

- -

Past-Tense Verbs

Make up a sentence about writing or writers with a present-tense or past-tense verb. Have a partner listen to your sentence and name the verb tense. Use words from the list below. Take turns making up sentences and listening for verbs and verb tenses.

like, liked	**work, worked**	**spell, spelled**
describe, described	**enjoy, enjoyed**	**report, reported**

Auditory

- -

Past-Tense Verbs

Write the words below on separate index cards. Place them in a paper bag. Sit in a circle with three or four partners, and pass the bag around the circle. Have each person choose a card and make up a sentence that includes the verb on the card. Have the other group members listen to the sentence and tell whether the verb is in the past tense or the present tense. Continue until all the verbs have been used.

research, researched	**like, liked**	**name, named**

Kinesthetic

- -

Teacher: Cut apart the activities and distribute to students based on the modalities that are their strengths.
(Visual) Have a volunteer write the past-tense paragraph on the board so that students can check their work.
(Auditory) Challenge students to make up a group story, using as many of the past-tense verbs from the list as they can.
(Kinesthetic) Extend the activity by having students sort the cards according to whether the verb is in the present tense or the past tense.

More About Past-Tense Verbs

Read the paragraph. If an underlined verb is in the past tense, put a check above it. If it is not, cross it out and write the past-tense form above it.

Jacob begged (✓) the librarian for a good mystery. He ~~hurry~~ *hurried* home to read the one she gave him. He ~~try~~ *tried* to guess the ending as he read. He imagined (✓) that he was a detective. He ~~solve~~ *solved* the mystery just before the last page.

Visual ✂

More About Past-Tense Verbs

Have a spelling bee with a small group of students.

Choose one group member to be the quizmaster. Have the quizmaster read aloud past-tense verbs from the *Pupil Edition* chapter. Take turns spelling the verbs aloud. Give one point each time a student spells a word correctly.

Auditory ✂

More About Past-Tense Verbs

Work in a group of four. Cut out the cards below and hand them out to three of the group members. Ask the fourth group member to read aloud past-tense verbs from the *Pupil Edition* chapter. After each verb is read, have the person with the card that tells its spelling rule stand and display the card. Take turns being the reader.

| Drop the *e* | Double the final consonant | Change *y* to *i* |

Kinesthetic ✂

Teacher: Cut apart the activities and distribute to students based on the modalities that are their strengths.
(Visual) Have students explain the rule they used to form the past-tense verbs.
(Auditory) After every five words, the speller with the most points becomes the new quizmaster.
(Kinesthetic) Have students tape the cards to the board and list past-tense verbs that belong in each category.

Reteach Activities • Past-Tense Verbs   Unit 3 • Chapter 14 29

Subject-Verb Agreement

Circle the sentence if the subject and verb agree. If they do not, rewrite the verb to make them agree.

(Do you like the *Ramona* books?) _____

Ramona and her family is funny. ___are___

Ramona always get into trouble. ___gets___

(Ramona worries about her problems.) _____

Along come her dad with the answer. ___comes___

Visual

Subject-Verb Agreement

With your partner, look through a favorite book. Read aloud sentences with a compound subject, with part of the predicate before the subject, or with other words between the subject and predicate. Together, identify the subject and the verb. If the subject and verb agree, you will know you are correct.

Auditory

Subject-Verb Agreement

Cut out the cards below. Place the correct verb in each sentence.

In	Zach and Tino.		
Marge with books in her arms		through the library door.	
Noel and Cleo	the same books.		
Noel	mysteries, too.		
like	rushes	likes	rush

Kinesthetic

Teacher: Cut apart the activities and distribute to students based on the modalities that are their strengths.
(Visual) Have students name the subject and verb in each sentence to check for agreement.
(Auditory) Have students write on sentence strips the sentences they find and display them on a bulletin board.
(Kinesthetic) Have students use the completed sentences as models for writing their own sentences.

30 Unit 3 • Chapter 14   Reteach Activities • Past-Tense Verbs

Future-Tense Verbs

Underline the past-tense verbs. Above each, write the verb in the future tense.

Joanna <u>played</u> the drums. [will play] In high school, she <u>joined</u> the marching band. [will join] The band <u>practiced</u> every day after school. [will practice] They <u>traveled</u> to California. [will travel] In California, they <u>marched</u> in a big parade. [will march]

Visual

Future-Tense Verbs

What was the name of that show?

Tell a partner the story from a stage or television show you have seen. Then retell the story, using future-tense verbs. Have your partner listen to make sure all your verbs are in the future tense. Then listen while your partner tells a story in the past and future tenses.

Auditory

Future-Tense Verbs

Plan a talent show with a small group of students. Decide what you would do in the talent show if it were really taking place. Write a sentence with a future-tense verb that explains your act and give it to another group member. Let that group member introduce your performance, also using a future-tense verb.

Kinesthetic

Teacher: Cut apart the activities and distribute to students based on the modalities that are their strengths.
(Visual) Have a volunteer read the future-tense paragraph aloud so that students can check their work.
(Auditory) Suggest that students tape record their stories and replay them to listen for future-tense verbs.
(Kinesthetic) If time allows, let volunteers perform a short act after they have been introduced.

Reteach Activities • Future-Tense Verbs   Unit 3 • Chapter 16   31

More About Future-Tense Verbs

Circle each future-tense verb. Put a check above any word that comes between *will* and the main verb.

The chorus (will) often (sing) folk songs.

The group (will) sometimes (perform) on stage.

(Will) you (play) some in our class?

Your parents (will) probably (know) these songs.

Visual

More About Future-Tense Verbs

With a partner, take turns reading aloud sentences from a book about music or musicians. For each sentence, name the verb. Then change the verb to the future tense and say the sentence with the future-tense verb. Point out any words that come between *will* and the main verb.

Auditory

More About Future-Tense Verbs

Write down a sentence about your favorite music or musician. Use a verb in the future tense and one of the words below. Have a partner point out the parts of the future-tense verb and circle with a finger any word or words that come between. Then switch roles.

    also   surely   probably   not

Kinesthetic

Teacher: Cut apart the activities and distribute to students based on the modalities that are their strengths.
(Visual) Have students name the subject in each sentence.
(Auditory) Suggest that to avoid complex sentences, students read from books written for young children.
(Kinesthetic) Have students write their sentences on the board, and tell them to cup their hands around the future-tense verbs.

32 Unit 3 • Chapter 16   Reteach Activities • Future-Tense Verbs

Choosing the Correct Tense

Cross out the verb tense error in each sentence. Above it, write the correct verb. Use the verb tense in parentheses.

practiced
Jeremy will practice the drum last week.   (past)

learned
Juanita learns a new song yesterday.   (past)

will play
Joanna played the guitar tomorrow.   (future)

started
Last week the four friends starts a band.   (past)

Visual

Choosing the Correct Tense

Do you like music?

Talk with a partner about your experiences with music. Tell about music you enjoyed in the past, music you enjoy now, and how you think music will be a part of your life in the future. Have your partner list the verbs you use and name the tense of each verb. Switch roles and listen to your partner.

Auditory

Choosing the Correct Tense

For a small group, act out playing a musical instrument.

Call out the name of a verb tense. Then call on a volunteer to make up a sentence about your actions, using the correct verb tense. Take turns performing and making up sentences.

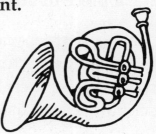

Kinesthetic

Teacher: Cut apart the activities and distribute to students based on the modalities that are their strengths.
(Visual) Have students change the sentences and put all verbs in the present tense.
(Auditory) Have students compile a list of the verbs they used, organizing the verbs according to tense.
(Kinesthetic) Suggest that the group begin by brainstorming a list of familiar musical instruments.

Reteach Activities • Future-Tense Verbs

Irregular Verbs

Proofread the paragraph. Cross out each incorrect irregular verb. Write the correct form of the verb above it.

    Grandma thinked [thought] it was time to clean out her attic. Andy and his cousins beginned [began] the job for her. "What strange clothes people weared [wore] in the old days!" Andy exclaimed. Andy looked at an old picture. At first, he thinked [thought] it was made by a child. He throwed [threw] it on the junk pile. Just then Grandma walked in. Andy bringed [brought] the picture out. "I knowed [knew] this was somewhere around," Grandma said. "It is not junk. It is valuable folk art."

Visual ✂

Irregular Verbs

What is folk art?

    Look through art books to find an example of folk art. Tell a partner a story about how you think the work was created. Use past-tense verbs. Have your partner listen and raise his or her hand each time you use an irregular verb. Then switch roles.

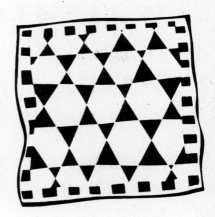

Auditory ✂

Irregular Verbs

Make a piece of artwork from clay.

    Have a partner watch you work. Exhibit the artwork while your partner tells a small group how you made it. Have the audience listen for irregular verbs and raise their hands each time they hear one. Take turns creating art, describing it, and listening for irregular verbs.

Kinesthetic

Teacher: Cut apart the activities and distribute to students based on the modalities that are their strengths.
(Visual) Have students write all three forms of the verbs they replaced.
(Auditory) Ask an observer to record the irregular verbs. Then have students name all the forms of each one.
(Kinesthetic) Ask an observer to record the irregular verbs. Then have students name all the forms of each one.

More Irregular Verbs

Proofread the cartoon dialogue below. Cross out incorrect irregular verbs or helping verbs. Write the correct word above the one you cross out.

Dog Jeff: The wind ~~have~~ *has* blown my doghouse down.

Dog Elmer: You don't say! The wind has ~~took~~ *taken* my tent, too.

Dog Jeff: This weather has ~~give~~ *given* us a hard time.

Dog Elmer: I said the weather was good. I ~~spoken~~ *spoke* too soon.

Visual

More Irregular Verbs

Cut a cartoon strip or panel from a newspaper.

Tell a partner what happened in the cartoon and what made it interesting or funny. Use as many past-tense irregular verbs with helping verbs as you can. Have your partner raise a hand each time he or she hears an irregular past-tense verb with a helping verb.

Auditory

More Irregular Verbs

With a partner or a small group, find a newspaper cartoon that you can perform.

Role play it, and have your audience use irregular past-tense verbs with helping verbs to explain your "living cartoon." Then display the cartoon on which you based your skit.

Kinesthetic

Teacher: Cut apart the activities and distribute to students based on the modalities that are their strengths.
(Visual) Ask students to draw the cartoon strip to match the dialogue.
(Auditory) Have students write down their synopses and post them on a bulletin board beside the cartoon.
(Kinesthetic) Students might enjoy videotaping their skits.

Reteach Activities • Irregular Verbs

Commonly Misused Verbs

Circle the correct verb form in parentheses.

The potter **(sits**, **sets)** in front of her wheel.

She **(lies**, **lays)** down some clay.

She **(raises**, **rises)** and lowers the foot pedal.

As the wheel spins, the sides of the pot **(rise**, **raise)**.

When the pot is formed, she **(sits, sets)** it in the kiln.

Visual

Commonly Misused Verbs

Say one of the verbs below aloud to your partner.

Have your partner make up a sentence that uses the verb correctly. Listen to make sure the sentence is correct. Give your partner ten points for a correct sentence. Take turns saying words and making up sentences.

| lie | lay | raise | rise | sit | set |

Auditory

Commonly Misused Verbs

Pick up a handy classroom object and sit in a chair.

Listen as your partner gives you commands that include the words *lie, lay, raise, rise, sit,* or *set*. Follow a command only if your partner uses the correct verb. Then switch roles.

Kinesthetic

Teacher: Cut apart the activities and distribute to students based on the modalities that are their strengths.
(Visual) Have students explain their verb choices.
(Auditory) Have a third student act as judge, using the chart in the *Pupil Edition* to confirm that sentences are correct.
(Kinesthetic) Play the game in a small group, using the rules for Simon Says.

Pronouns and Pronoun Antecedents

Underline the pronoun. Draw an arrow from each pronoun to its antecedent. Tell whether the pronoun and its antecedent are singular or plural.

Some people say they love the rain. _____plural_____

"I like to stay indoors and watch the storm," says Tosh. _____singular_____

"Benny and Bill, do you jump and splash in puddles?" _____plural_____

Jessie says a cold rain makes her sneeze. _____singular_____

Visual

Pronouns and Pronoun Antecedents

In magazines or textbooks, look for pictures that show people or objects or groups of people or objects. Show one of the pictures to a partner. Have your partner name at least one pronoun whose antecedent could be the people or objects in the picture.

Auditory

Pronouns and Pronoun Antecedents

Work with a small group of students to write the pronouns from the chart in the *Pupil Edition* on index cards. Place the cards face down and take turns choosing a card. The student who picked the card must cut out a picture from an old magazine as an example of objects or people, or groups of objects or people, for which the pronoun could stand. Display the pictures matched to the pronoun cards for the group.

Kinesthetic

Teacher: Cut apart the activities and distribute to students based on the modalities that are their strengths.
(Visual) Have students write their own sentences or pairs of sentences that show correct use of pronouns and their antecedents.
(Auditory) Have students use the pronoun they name in a sentence about the picture.
(Kinesthetic) Have students write words that name objects, people, or groups on index cards and match pronoun cards with antecedent cards.

Reach Activities • Pronouns   Unit 4 • Chapter 19   37

Subject and Object Pronouns

Underline the pronoun in each sentence. Write whether it is a subject or an object pronoun. If the sentence has an object pronoun, draw an arrow from the action verb to the object pronoun.

Last January <u>we</u> had a huge snowstorm.   _subject_

<u>It</u> lasted for three long days and three long nights.   _subject_

The heavy snow kept <u>us</u> indoors for a whole week.   _object_

Snowplows got through the streets and cleared <u>them</u>.   _object_

Visual

Subject and Object Pronouns

Have you ever been in a big storm?

Take turns reading from a book about any kind of big storm. At the end of each sentence, pause to let your partner name pronouns in the sentence and tell whether they are subject or object pronouns.

Auditory

Subject and Object Pronouns

What would you do if you were in a bad rainstorm?

With a partner, make up a skit about what you might do if you were caught in a bad rainstorm. Perform your skit for a small group. Make up dialogue as you do your skit. Ask a volunteer to list the pronouns you use. After your skit is over, have the recorder read the list aloud. Tell whether each pronoun is a subject or an object pronoun.

Kinesthetic

Teacher: Cut apart the activities and distribute to students based on the modalities that are their strengths.
(Visual) Ask students to write about a storm experience. Then have them trade papers to locate the subject and object pronouns.
(Auditory) Have students use pronouns as they tell each other what they learned from their reading.
(Kinesthetic) Recap by having students name the subject pronouns and then the object pronouns.

Using *I* and *Me*; *We* and *Us*

Decide if the underlined pronoun in each sentence is correct. If it is incorrect, cross it out and write the correct pronoun above it.

    I
Me like to play outdoors in sunny weather, but a gloomy day can be fun, too. On gloomy days, I sit by the fire. My best friend comes over, and I share our favorite books. Sometimes my friend reads a good part aloud to I. At lunch time, Mom makes hot soup for we. Then us play games until dinner time. After a quiet day, I feel rested and ready to run and play outdoors.

(Corrections: we over "I share"; me over "to I"; us over "we"; we over "us")

Visual ✂

Using *I* and *Me*; *We* and *Us*

What do you do on a rainy day?

Tell how you and a friend pass the time indoors on a day when the weather is stormy. Use each of the pronouns *I*, *me*, *we*, and *us* at least once. Have your partner listen and clap when he or she hears one of the four pronouns. Then listen for pronouns as your partner speaks.

Auditory ✂

Using *I* and *Me*; *We* and *Us*

Play a pronoun game.

Form a small group, and have each group member write these pronouns on separate index cards: *I, me, we, us*. Tape all the cards on the floor to make a path. Take turns throwing a die and moving that number of cards. When you stop, make up a sentence that includes the pronoun you are standing on.

Kinesthetic ✂

Teacher: Cut apart the activities and distribute to students based on the modalities that are their strengths.
(Visual) Ask a volunteer to read the corrected paragraph aloud so that other students can check their answers.
(Auditory) Students may enjoy illustrating their stories and displaying their illustrations as they speak.
(Kinesthetic) Make the game more exciting; have students add extra cards for penalties, such as "Lose a turn" or "Move back three steps."

Reteach Activities • Pronouns

Possessive Pronouns

Read each sentence and underline the possessive pronoun. Then draw an arrow from the pronoun to the noun that follows it.

Jody and Mike went to visit their aunt.

Her home is out in the country.

One night, Jody lay on his back and looked up at the stars.

"Our stars are bright tonight, Mike," he said.

Visual

Possessive Pronouns

Play I Spy with a partner. Choose an object that is in plain sight. Don't tell what it is. Give your partner two clues. One clue should include an adjective that describes the object: *I spy something that is round.* The other should include a possessive pronoun to tell who owns the object: *It is yours.* Let your partner ask questions about the object that can be answered with *yes* or *no*. To guess what the object is, your partner must use a possessive pronoun: *Is it my watch?* Switch roles and continue playing.

Auditory

Possessive Pronouns

With a partner, write these possessive pronouns on self-stick notes. Take a walk around the classroom and label objects with the notes. Try to use all the pronouns. Say aloud the pronoun and noun, such as "My shirt," as you stick on the note.

my	her	their	theirs
your	its	mine	hers
his	our	yours	ours

Kinesthetic

Teacher: Cut apart the activities and distribute to students based on the modalities that are their strengths.
(Visual) Have students explain the difference between *their* and *our*.
(Auditory) Students may use the pronoun chart in the *Pupil Edition* chapter for help.
(Kinesthetic) Remind students that some pronouns, such as *my, yours, ours,* and *theirs*, depend on the speaker's point of view.

40 Unit 4 • Chapter 20   Reteach Activities • More About Pronouns

Contractions with Pronouns

In each sentence, find two words that can be turned into a contraction. Underline the two words and write above them the contraction you make.

Ted and Anna study because <u>they would</u> like to be astronauts. *(they'd)*

<u>He is</u> planning to be a space shuttle pilot. *(He's)*

Do you think <u>they will</u> succeed? *(they'll)*

<u>I am</u> sure Ted and Anna will achieve their goals. *(I'm)*

<u>You are</u> sure that they will, too. *(You're)*

Visual

- -

Contractions with Pronouns

What does an astronaut do?

Tell your partner something you know about astronauts or space. Use contractions. Ask your partner to listen and to clap whenever you use a contraction that includes a pronoun. Take turns listening and speaking.

Auditory

- -

Contractions with Pronouns

Write the contractions and phrases below on index cards. Mix them up and turn them face down. With a partner, take turns choosing two cards at a time. If you turn up a contraction and the words it stands for, keep the cards. Continue matching cards until all the cards are gone.

I'm	it's	we've	you'd	you'll	he's	they'd
I am	it is	we have	you would	you will	he has	they had

Kinesthetic

- -

Teacher: Cut apart the activities and distribute to students based on the modalities that are their strengths.
(Visual) Have students exchange papers and check the contractions.
(Auditory) Ask a third student to record the contractions. Afterward, students can name the words that make up each contraction.
(Kinesthetic) Have students pick up the cards one at a time. They can make a contraction from the phrases and tell the words for which the contractions stand.

Reteach Activities • More About Pronouns

Homophones

Read each sentence. If the homophone is incorrect, cross it out and write the correct one.

Look at the sky chart in ~~you're~~ your science book.

You'll find many familiar constellations ~~their~~ there.

Constellations get their names from old stories.

Your homework assignment is to look at the sky.

Visual

Homophones

Use one of these commonly confused words in a sentence. Have your partner listen for the homophone and spell it. Take turns making up sentences and spelling the homophones correctly.

their	your	its
they're	you're	it's
there		

Auditory

Homophones

In a small group, cut out large construction-paper stars. Write one of the homophones below on each star, and tape the stars to the floor to make a path. Place a round moon at the end of the path. Take turns walking along the path. Stop on each star, and use the homophone on the star in a sentence. Can you reach the moon without making a mistake?

| their | they're | there | |
| your | you're | its | it's |

Kinesthetic

Teacher: Cut apart the activities and distribute to students based on the modalities that are their strengths.
(Visual) Have students write sentences using *you're, they're, it's,* and *its* correctly.
(Auditory) After each sentence, have students explain their reasons for choosing the homophone.
(Kinesthetic) Give one star to each student. Say a sentence with one homophone. Have the student who has the star hold it up.

42 Unit 4 • Chapter 20   Reteach Activities • More About Pronouns

Adjectives

Underline the adjectives in the paragraph. Draw an arrow from each adjective to the noun it describes.

Last winter, I planned a garden. I looked in colorful catalogs. In the spring, I dug up the hard dirt. I planted little seeds and covered them with earth. I watered the ground and waited. Soon tiny green sprouts popped up. By July, beautiful flowers filled the yard.

-- Visual ✂

Adjectives

Which plants are beautiful?

Find pictures of colorful plants in an old magazine. With a partner, brainstorm a list of adjectives you could use to describe each picture. Then make up a long sentence with many adjectives to describe one of the pictures. See if you and your partner can repeat the long sentence.

-- Auditory ✂

Adjectives

What do you know about plants?

Work with two or three other students. Each of you write five adjectives and one noun naming a plant on separate index cards. Have a group leader stand in front of the group and show a noun card. Anyone who has an adjective that could describe the noun stands beside the leader. Take turns being leader.

-- Kinesthetic ✂

Teacher: Cut apart the activities and distribute to students based on the modalities that are their strengths.
(Visual) Have students tell whether each adjective tells *what kind, how many,* or *which one,* or is an article.
(Auditory) Tell students to cut out and glue their pictures on construction paper and write the sentences below as captions.
(Kinesthetic) Have students sort the group's adjective cards according to what they tell about the noun.

Reteach Activities • Adjectives and Adverbs   Unit 4 • Chapter 22   43

Adverbs

Draw an arrow from the underlined adverb to the verb it describes. On the line after the sentence, write *where, when,* or *how.*

<u>Yesterday</u> we heard a loud crash.   when

The big tree in our front yard had fallen <u>down</u>.   where

You can <u>easily</u> tell the age of a fallen tree.   how

I <u>carefully</u> counted the rings in the stump.   how

Visual

Adverbs

Sit in a circle with a small group of other students.

Say a sentence that includes an adverb. Have group members listen and raise their hands when they hear the adverb. Call on a group member to name the adverb and to say whether it tells *when, where,* or *how* the action was done. Then another group member takes a turn saying a sentence with an adverb.

Auditory

Adverbs

Think of an action verb, such as *walk*. Say the verb, along with an adverb that tells *how: walk slowly.* Have your partner act out your instructions. Change the adverb and have your partner change his or her actions. Take turns acting out new verbs and adverbs.

Kinesthetic

Teacher: Cut apart the activities and distribute to students based on the modalities that are their strengths.
(Visual) Remind students that some verbs consist of a helping verb and a main verb. An adverb modifies the whole verb phrase.
(Auditory) Afterward, students can write their sentences on the board and circle the adverbs.
(Kinesthetic) Remind students that many adverbs that tell *how* end in *ly.*

44   Unit 4 • Chapter 22   Reteach Activities • Adjectives and Adverbs

Adjective or Adverb?

Draw an arrow from the underlined word to the word it describes. Write *adjective* or *adverb* on the line.

Sara felt good when she saw the garden.   adjective

Unfortunately, the roses were growing badly.   adverb

The bad weather had turned them brown.   adjective

The daylilies were doing well, though.   adverb

Visual

Adjective or Adverb?

With your group, write *adjective* on five index cards and *adverb* on five other index cards. Place all ten cards in a bag. Sit in a circle and pass the bag around. Each student draws a card from the bag, shows it to the group, and makes up a sentence that has the kind of word the card names. The other students listen to the sentence and name the adjective or adverb.

Auditory

Adjective or Adverb?

Put a piece of masking tape on each side of a square block.

On the pieces of tape, write *good, well, bad, badly, any adjective,* and *any adverb*. Take turns rolling the block back and forth. After each roll, the student with the block must make up a sentence that includes the word or type of word that is on top of the block.

Kinesthetic

Teacher: Cut apart the activities and distribute to students based on the modalities that are their strengths.
(Visual) Ask students to explain how they decided whether each word was an adjective or adverb.
(Auditory) Students may use sentences from the *Pupil Edition* as models, if necessary.
(Kinesthetic) Tell a third student to look in the *Pupil Edition* to decide whether each sentence is correct.

Reteach Activities • Adjectives and Adverbs   Unit 4 • Chapter 22   45

Other Kinds of Adverbs

Circle the word the underlined adverb modifies. Write whether the word you circled is an adjective or adverb.

Blake is quite (grateful) for icy Diamond Lake.   _adjective_

That's because he is very (happy) in the water.   _adjective_

Most (willingly), Blake joined a swim club.   _adverb_

Even in winter, they dive in very (cheerfully).   _adverb_

Visual

Other Kinds of Adverbs

Say a phrase that includes an adjective or adverb, such as *high mountains* or *moved quickly*. Ask your partner to listen and then repeat the phrase, adding an adverb that modifies the adjective or adverb, such as *very high mountains* or *moved too quickly*. Take turns saying and expanding the phrases.

Auditory

Other Kinds of Adverbs

Write these phrases on sentence strips. Put two strips together to form a sentence. Add an adverb between the two sentence parts. Write it on an index card. Tell what word the adverb modifies and whether the modified word is an adjective or adverb.

The Ice Age caused	thick ice sheets to form.
It also gave us	deep lakes.
Glaciers moved	slowly across the ground.

Kinesthetic

Teacher: Cut apart the activities and distribute to students based on the modalities that are their strengths.
(Visual) Students may find it easier to decide on the part of speech if they reread the sentence without the underlined word.
(Auditory) Let students use their *Pupil Editions* to find adverbs to use.
(Kinesthetic) Suggest that students try several different adverbs in each sentence.

Reteach Activities • More About Adjectives and Adverbs

Comparing with Adjectives and Adverbs

Read each sentence. Underline the comparative form of the adjective or adverb. Write the correct form above it.

Rocky River is <u>widest</u> than Stone Creek. *(wider)*

Of all the rivers here, the Poe is the <u>longer</u>. *(longest)*

Muddy Creek flows <u>most quickly</u> than Stone Creek. *(more)*

The <u>more dangerous</u> rapids of all are at the old mill. *(most)*

 Visual

Comparing with Adjectives and Adverbs

What do you see?

Look out the window with a partner. Talk together about what you see. Use adjectives or adverbs to compare things you see outside. Take turns making comparisons. After each comparison, name the adjective or adverb and tell what things you compared.

 Auditory

Comparing with Adjectives and Adverbs

With a partner, brainstorm adjectives and adverbs you could use to talk about nature.

Fold index cards in half. On the outside of each card, write an adjective or adverb in a form that compares two or more things or actions. On the inside, write whether the word is an adjective or adverb and the number of things it compares. Trade cards with your partner and test yourself.

 Kinesthetic

Teacher: Cut apart the activities and distribute to students based on the modalities that are their strengths.
(Visual) Have students make up other comparative sentences that tell about their neighborhoods.
(Auditory) If looking out windows is not practical, students might look at magazine photos.
(Kinesthetic) Have students write some of the words in sentences on the board and cup their hands around the adjectives or adverbs.

Reteach Activities • More About Adjectives and Adverbs   Unit 4 • Chapter 23   47

Special Forms

Add the correct forms of the adjectives and adverbs in the chart.

	Comparing Two	Comparing Three or More
Adjectives		
good	better	best
bad	worse	worst
little	less	least
Adverbs		
well	better	best
far	farther	farthest

Visual

Special Forms

Make up a sentence that includes one of the adjectives or adverbs in the box. Have your partner listen and then change the sentence slightly by using the form of the word that compares two things or the form that compares more than two. Remember that your partner may have to make a few other changes, too. Take turns making up and changing sentences.

| good | bad | well | badly |

Auditory

Special Forms

Write the words below on index cards. Shuffle them, and deal four cards each to yourself and a partner. If three of your cards are different forms of the same word, lay them face up in front of you and draw a card. If you cannot make a set, draw a card. Take turns until the draw pile is gone. Some words can be used in more than one way.

good	bad	well	badly
better	worse	better	worse
best	worst	best	worst

Kinesthetic

Teacher: Cut apart the activities and distribute to students based on the modalities that are their strengths.
(Visual) Have students check each other's charts.
(Auditory) If time allows, let students continue until they have used all the words at least once.
(Kinesthetic) After the game, have students take turns choosing a card and telling the other two forms of the word on the card.

48 Unit 4 • Chapter 23   Reteach Activities • More About Adjectives and Adverbs

Prepositions

Read the paragraph and underline the prepositions.

Cassidy takes the train into the city. She gazes at displays in the store windows. After shopping for a new coat, she goes to a restaurant. The restaurant is on the top floor of a store. She spends the rest of the day walking through a museum. Just before dinner time, Cassidy heads home.

Prepositions

Play a guessing game with a partner.

Choose an object in plain sight. Don't tell what it is. Instead, give a clue that includes a preposition, such as *It is over the door*. If your partner cannot guess the object, give another clue, such as *It is beside the flag*. Continue giving clues until your partner guesses correctly. Then let your partner give clues about another object while you guess.

Prepositions

Place one of your books on a chair. Make up a sentence that includes a preposition and tells about the book, such as *The book is on the chair*. Have your partner identify the preposition, move the book to another position, and make up a new sentence. Continue moving the book and making up sentences until you cannot think of any more prepositions.

Teacher: Cut apart the activities and distribute to students based on the modalities that are their strengths.
(Visual) Let students compare their paragraphs to check their answers.
(Auditory) Have a third student make a list of the prepositions used in the clues.
(Kinesthetic) Suggest that students make a list of the prepositions they use. Students can reread the list and count the prepositions.

Reteach Activities • Prepositions

Object of the Preposition

Read the paragraph. Underline the prepositions and draw arrows to the objects of the prepositions. Some sentences may have more than one preposition.

Have you ever flown <u>over</u> a big city <u>in</u> an airplane? At night, you can see lights <u>on</u> many buildings. You may see a big crowd <u>inside</u> a stadium. Cars and buses <u>on</u> the streets look very small. When an airplane flies <u>over</u> your head, look <u>into</u> the sky and imagine what the passengers see.

Visual

Object of the Preposition

Where would you like to visit?

Read aloud to a partner from a guidebook about a city you would enjoy visiting. Ask your partner to listen for prepositions. After each sentence, pause to let your partner name the prepositions and their objects. Then switch roles.

Auditory

Object of the Preposition

Make up directions for a partner.

Each direction should include a preposition and an object of the preposition. For example, *Sit on the floor, Walk through the door, Go up the stairs*. Have your partner follow the directions and then name the preposition and its object. Take turns giving directions and following them.

Kinesthetic

Teacher: Cut apart the activities and distribute to students based on the modalities that are their strengths.
(Visual) Students might enjoy illustrating the paragraph.
(Auditory) With your librarian's help, assemble a small collection of guidebooks in advance.
(Kinesthetic) Make sure students understand that they must stay in the room and pretend to follow directions that involve doors or stairs.

50 Unit 5 • Chapter 25   Reteach Activities • Prepositions

Using Prepositional Phrases

Draw a line from each sentence beginning to the prepositional phrase that best completes the sentence.

Many people go to work — with other drivers.

Some people carpool — to their offices.

A lot of workers take trains — in large cities.

Ferries transport some people — after a week of commuting.

Most people are tired — across the water.

Visual

Using Prepositional Phrases

What is there to do in a big city?

Say a short sentence about something you might do in a city. Have your partner expand the sentence by adding a prepositional phrase. Then see if you can make the sentence even more detailed by adding another prepositional phrase. When you complete one sentence, begin another.

Auditory

Using Prepositional Phrases

In a small group, pantomime something that happens in a big city.

Call on a volunteer in the group to say a sentence with a prepositional phrase to describe what you are doing. Call on another volunteer to identify the prepositional phrase. Then choose another actor and continue the activity.

Kinesthetic

Teacher: Cut apart the activities and distribute to students based on the modalities that are their strengths.
(Visual) Allow time for students to compare their answers.
(Auditory) Have students write out their longest sentence to share with the class.
(Kinesthetic) Students might begin by brainstorming activities to pantomime.

Reteach Activities • Prepositions   Unit 5 • Chapter 25   51

Independent Clauses

If the group of words is an independent clause, draw a circle around it. Then add any capital letters and punctuation marks that are needed. Draw a line under a phrase.

(my grandparents live in Ohio)   (they would miss the snow and ice)

enjoy the changing seasons   many people probably

won't move to Florida

Visual

Independent Clauses

Where do you live?

Say a phrase about the area where you live. Challenge your partner to turn the phrase into an independent clause by adding words. Say the independent clause together. Take turns saying phrases and making independent clauses.

Auditory

Independent Clauses

Think about your neighborhood.

On sentence strips, write five sentences about the area where you live. Cut each sentence apart into phrases. Place one part of each sentence in a box. Challenge your partner to choose a phrase from the box and match it with its missing part to form an independent clause.

Kinesthetic

Teacher: Cut apart the activities and distribute to students based on the modalities that are their strengths.
(Visual) Have students complete the phrases.
(Auditory) Have students draw a picture of a place where they live and write an independent clause as a caption.
(Kinesthetic) This activity can be done in a small group.

Reteach Activities • Phrases and Clauses

Dependent Clauses

Underline the dependent clause in each sentence. Circle the connecting word.

(When) my family moved to the North from Florida, I was unhappy.

I wanted to live (where) it was always warm and sunny.

I stayed unhappy (until) I saw the first snowfall.

I was excited (because) I had never seen snow.

Visual

Dependent Clauses

What do you know about your state?

Read aloud a paragraph from a book about your state. Have your partner raise one hand when he or she hears a dependent clause. Pause in your reading so that your partner can repeat the dependent clause and name the connecting word. Take turns reading and listening.

Auditory

Dependent Clauses

Share a book about your state with a partner.

Read a paragraph silently. Then read the same paragraph aloud together. One of you should read the independent clauses, and the other should read the dependent clauses. Each partner should stand up as he or she begins reading.

Kinesthetic

Teacher: Cut apart the activities and distribute to students based on the modalities that are their strengths.
(Visual) Have students explain their answers.
(Auditory) Let students look through the *Pupil Edition* to make a list of connecting words.
(Kinesthetic) If possible, students can use two books that are alike instead of sharing one book.

Reteach Activities • Phrases and Clauses

Distinguishing Independent and Dependent Clauses

Read each sentence. Draw a line between the independent and the dependent clause. Underline the independent clause once and the dependent clause twice.

Because Laura Ingalls Wilder was a pioneer, | her books tell about an important part of our history.

Sometimes the family moved | because the crops failed.

Visual

Distinguishing Independent and Dependent Clauses

Have you ever met a cowboy?

    Make up a dependent clause about pioneers or cowboys. Say the dependent clause and ask your partner to complete the sentence by adding an independent clause. Take turns saying dependent clauses and adding independent clauses.

Auditory

Distinguishing Independent and Dependent Clauses

Form a group of four students. Write the clauses below on sentence strips. Give each group member one strip. Then each student reads his or her clause and makes up an independent or a dependent clause to form a sentence that makes sense.

because they could not get to a doctor.   **Because life was hard for pioneers,**

if they were to survive.   **many did not survive.**

Kinesthetic

Teacher: Cut apart the activities and distribute to students based on the modalities that are their strengths.
(Visual) Have students circle the connecting word that signals a dependent clause in each sentence.
(Auditory) Ask students to tell how they know a clause is dependent.
(Kinesthetic) Remind students that each complete sentence will have both an independent and a dependent clause.

54 Unit 5 • Chapter 26   Reteach Activities • Phrases and Clauses

Complex Sentences

Draw one line under the independent clause in each complex sentence. Draw two lines under the dependent clause.

<u>The Great Lakes are important</u> <u><u>because they are a shipping route</u></u>.

<u><u>When summer comes</u></u>, <u>the lakes are filled with boats</u>.

<u>Boaters sail around all day</u> <u><u>as they visit the islands</u></u>.

<u><u>If you are planning a vacation</u></u>, <u>you should consider the Great Lakes</u>.

Visual

Complex Sentences

Where would you like to go on vacation?

Tell a partner a good reason for planning a vacation in your area. Use a compound or a complex sentence. Have your partner listen, tell whether the sentence is compound or complex, and explain how he or she knows. Then switch roles.

Auditory

Complex Sentences

On a sentence strip, write a complex or compound sentence telling a good reason to vacation in your area or state.

With other group members, arrange your sentences to make sense in a brochure for tourists. Then tell whether each sentence is compound or complex.

Kinesthetic

Teacher: Cut apart the activities and distribute to students based on the modalities that are their strengths.
(Visual) Have students explain their answers.
(Auditory) For each sentence, have students explain their answers.
(Kinesthetic) Students might enjoy drawing pictures to illustrate their ideas.

Reteach Activities • Complex Sentences

More About Complex Sentences

Read each complex sentence. Circle the word that connects the two clauses.

You should eat fruits and vegetables (because) they are healthful for you.

You can grow your own vegetables (if) you want.

Prepare the soil (after) the ground thaws.

You must water the seeds (unless) you have plenty of rain.

Visual

More About Complex Sentences

How do you care for a garden?

With a partner, give directions for planting and caring for a plant or a garden. Say an independent clause. Have your partner turn it into a complex sentence by adding a dependent clause. Take turns starting and completing sentences.

Auditory

More About Complex Sentences

Write the connecting words below on separate index cards. Shuffle them and place them face down in a pile. With a partner, take turns drawing a card and using the word in a complex sentence about gardening or growing plants.

because	when	since
if	until	although

Kinesthetic

Teacher: Cut apart the activities and distribute to students based on the modalities that are their strengths.
(Visual) Have students read aloud the connecting word they found for each sentence.
(Auditory) Before students begin, have them brainstorm words about gardening or growing plants.
(Kinesthetic) After the activity, have students name all the connecting words they can recall.

Commas in Complex Sentences

If the sentence does not need a comma, put a check next to it. Add commas where necessary.

When the twentieth century began, many people worked on farms.

People left the farms because they wanted to work in factories. ✓

Remaining farmers traded horses for tractors so they could farm more efficiently. ✓

Although farming is still important, there are fewer farms today.

Visual

Commas in Complex Sentences

Make up a complex sentence about farming that does not need a comma. Say your sentence aloud, and have your partner listen and repeat it. Challenge your partner to change the sentence so that it needs a comma. When your partner says the new sentence, he or she must say "comma" at the place where the comma belongs.

Auditory

Commas in Complex Sentences

Draw a comma on an index card.

With a partner, locate a book about farming. Take turns finding a complex sentence in the book and reading it aloud. The partner who is listening holds up the comma card if the sentence should have a comma.

Kinesthetic

Teacher: Cut apart the activities and distribute to students based on the modalities that are their strengths.
(Visual) Have students explain how they decided a comma was needed.
(Auditory) Students can write one pair of sentences, compare the two versions, and explain why one has a comma and the other does not.
(Kinesthetic) Have students write the sentences that need commas and place the comma card in the right spot.

Reteach Activities • Complex Sentences   Unit 5 • Chapter 28   57

Sentence Fragments

Draw a line under each sentence. Circle each fragment.

Some zoos have built rain forest habitats.

(Automatic rainstorm every hour on the hour.)

(Insects below the ground in cages with glass walls.)

Birds flutter through the canopy.

You can experience a rain forest without traveling.

Visual

Sentence Fragments

What do you know about rain forests?

Read to a partner from a book about a rain forest. Either read a complete sentence, or read part of a sentence, leaving out the subject or the predicate. Have your partner listen and tell whether the group of words is a sentence or a fragment. Take turns reading and listening.

Auditory

Sentence Fragments

What do you know about rain forests?

On separate sentence strips, write a subject, a predicate, and a complete sentence. Use rain forests as your topic. Mix your sentence strips together with the sentence strips of two or three other students. Sort the strips according to whether they are fragments or complete sentences.

Kinesthetic

Teacher: Cut apart the activities and distribute to students based on the modalities that are their strengths.
(Visual) Have students tell what is missing from each fragment.
(Auditory) Have the listeners turn the fragments into complete sentences and compare them with the originals.
(Kinesthetic) Have students tell what is missing from each fragment.

58 Unit 5 • Chapter 29   Reteach Activities • Sentence Fragments and Run-on Sentences

Run-on Sentences

Circle each correct sentence. Underline each run-on sentence.

Egypt is an ancient land its tombs and artifacts are interesting.

Archaeologists studied the tombs, they learned about ancient Egypt.

(The most famous tomb of all was the tomb of King Tut.)

(King Tut was called "the boy king" because he was so young when he died.)

He was a young king he was an important king, too.

Visual

Run-on Sentences

What would you like to know about Egypt?

Read aloud from a book about Egypt. Choose one long sentence that is correct, or choose two shorter sentences and read them together as one sentence. Do not pause for the period between them. Have your partner listen and tell whether the sentence you read is correct or a run-on sentence.

Auditory

Run-on Sentences

On separate sentence strips, write a run-on sentence about Egypt and a long, correct sentence about Egypt.

Trade sentence strips with a partner. Read the sentences and separate the correct sentence from the run-on sentence. With a pencil or marker, fix the run-on sentence by inserting the period. Make other necessary changes.

Kinesthetic

Teacher: Cut apart the activities and distribute to students based on the modalities that are their strengths.
(Visual) Have students tell how to correct the run-on sentences.
(Auditory) Ask how students recognized the run-on sentences.
(Kinesthetic) Students can complete this activity in a small group.

Reteach Activities • Sentence Fragments and Run-on Sentences

Correcting Sentence Errors

Write whether each group of words is a sentence fragment or a run-on sentence. Rewrite each sentence correctly. Rewritten sentences may vary.

Mark Twain is a famous author he wrote funny stories. _____ run-on

Mark Twain is a famous author. He wrote funny stories.

Loved the Mississippi River most of all. _____ fragment

Twain loved the Mississippi River most of all.

Visual

- ✂

Correcting Sentence Errors

What can you find out about rivers?

Read aloud a sentence from a book about rivers. Change the sentence as you read to make it a sentence fragment or a run-on sentence. Have your partner listen and correct the sentence. Compare your partner's sentence to the original version. Take turns reading and correcting sentences.

Auditory

- ✂

Correcting Sentence Errors

Sit in a circle with a group of classmates and pass around a pencil.

The person holding the pencil says an incorrect sentence and hands the pencil to any other person in the group. That person must tell whether the group of words is a sentence fragment or a run-on sentence. When group members agree that the answer is right, pass the pencil along to another person who makes up a new incorrect sentence.

Kinesthetic

- ✂

Teacher: Cut apart the activities and distribute to students based on the modalities that are their strengths.
(Visual) Have students compare their answers to find several ways each incorrect sentence could be corrected.
(Auditory) Ask each listener to explain his or her answer.
(Kinesthetic) Continue until every group member has had at least one chance to correct a sentence.

60 Unit 5 • Chapter 29 Reteach Activities • Sentence Fragments and Run-on Sentences

Commas

Circle the sentence in each pair that is correctly punctuated with commas.

Danny would you like to go on a camping trip?
(Danny, would you like to go on a camping trip?)

(Omar and Bartolo, my cousins, are coming along.)
Omar and Bartolo, my cousins are coming along.

We will hike, fish, and sleep, in a tent.
(We will hike, fish, and sleep in a tent.)

Visual

Commas

Have you ever been camping?

Read aloud from a book about camping a sentence that has at least one comma. When you come to a comma, read it aloud as if it were a word. For example, you might say "We need a tent comma some food comma and warm clothes." Have your partner listen and explain why each comma is necessary. Then switch roles.

Auditory

Commas

With a partner, make up a skit about asking an adult for permission to go on a camping trip. In your dialogue, use a series of nouns or verbs, introductory words, nouns of direct address, and appositives. Perform your skit for an audience. Have your listeners punctuate your skit by clapping once whenever a comma is needed.

Kinesthetic

Teacher: Cut apart the activities and distribute to students based on the modalities that are their strengths.
(Visual) Have students correct the commas in the incorrect sentences.
(Auditory) Gather a selection of camping books in advance.
(Kinesthetic) Have students look in the *Pupil Edition* for examples of where commas are needed.

Reteach Activities • Commas and Colons   Unit 6 • Chapter 31   61

Colons

Correct the letter. Add colons or change incorrect punctuation to colons.

Dear Mr. Eli:

   I am writing to request a reservation at your campground for the first week in July. We will be there on the following days, Tuesday, Wednesday, and Thursday. We will arrive around 1000 Tuesday morning. We'll be leaving at 400 Thursday afternoon. We need these things, one large camping space, a water hookup, and an electrical hookup.

                                            Yours truly,
                                            Julia Smith

Visual

Colons

Suppose that you are the boss of a sporting goods company. Dictate to your partner a short business letter. Speak slowly so that your partner can write down what you say. Include a time and a list in your letter. Check your partner's use of colons. Then let your partner dictate a letter to you.

Auditory

Colons

Draw a colon on an index card. Then take turns with a partner making up sentences about camping. Use lists and times in some of your sentences. Have your partner hold up the colon card if your sentence needs a colon.

Kinesthetic

Teacher: Cut apart the activities and distribute to students based on the modalities that are their strengths.
(Visual) Tell students that colons are also used after the greeting of a business letter.
(Auditory) Tell students that colons are also used after the greeting of a business letter.
(Kinesthetic) If time allows, have students write their sentences on sentence strips and insert the colon card where it is needed.

Commas Versus Colons

Circle the correct letter. Add commas and colons to correct the other.

Dear Mr. Wilson:
    This is to agree that we will meet in Dallas,Texas. I will see you July 10,at 400.

        Sincerely,

        Ralph Jones

> Dear Grandma,
>   I will see you Sunday at 11:00. We can bake cookies, play, and go to the park.
>
>   Love,
>
>   Jack

Visual

Commas Versus Colons

Cut out the cards below. Work with a small group of students. Take turns saying a sentence or other group of words that needs commas, a colon, or both. After each sentence, have the listeners hold up one or both cards to show what kind of punctuation is needed. The speaker may call on a listener to tell where the punctuation mark or marks belong.

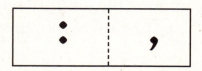

Auditory

Commas Versus Colons

Work with two other students. Write on the board a group of words that needs commas or colons. Leave out the commas or colons. A second student uses a pointer or ruler to point to places in the word group where punctuation is needed. The third student writes in the missing punctuation marks. Rotate jobs after each round.

Kinesthetic

Teacher: Cut apart the activities and distribute to students based on the modalities that are their strengths.
(Visual) Have a volunteer write the corrected letter on the board.
(Auditory) Suggest students use groups of words from the *Pupil Edition* as models. Ask them why colons and commas are needed.
(Kinesthetic) Students might enjoy writing on transparencies instead of the board.

Reteach Activities • Commas and Colons   Unit 6 • Chapter 31   63

Underlining and Using Quotation Marks in Titles

Circle the correct sentence. Correct the punctuation of titles in the rest.

Our book club's next selection is "My Horse Thunder."

(Sometimes our club reads magazines like Stories for Kids.)

So far, our favorite story is "Fourth Grade Can Be Tough."

To end every meeting, we sing our theme song, "Reading Is Cool."

Visual

Underlining and Using Quotation Marks in Titles

What do you like to read?

Talk about your favorite reading materials with a partner. Listen for titles. When you hear a title that should be underlined, trace a line in the air. If the title needs quotation marks, hold up the first two fingers on each hand.

Auditory

Underlining and Using Quotation Marks in Titles

Take a survey. Make forms with items like the ones below. Survey two people. Fill in the forms and compare them.

Favorite Book: _____

Favorite Short Story: _____

Favorite Song: _____

Kinesthetic

Teacher: Cut apart the activities and distribute to students based on the modalities that are their strengths.
(Visual) Extend the activity by having students list reading materials they would talk about in a reading club.
(Auditory) Allow students to share their favorite titles with other classmates.
(Kinesthetic) If time is limited, have students work in pairs to survey each other.

Capitalizing Words in Titles

Circle the correct title in each pair.

too Many Cats!
(Too Many Cats!)

the Big Lion and the little lion
(The Big Lion and the Little Lion)

("I've Been Workin' on the Railroad")
"I've Been Workin' On The Railroad"

Soccer is for Everyone
(Soccer Is for Everyone)

Capitalizing Words in Titles

Can you name your favorite things?

Say the title of a favorite book, story, magazine, poem, or song. Have your partner repeat the title, standing while saying words that should be capitalized and sitting while saying words that should not be capitalized. Take turns saying titles and repeating them.

Capitalizing Words in Titles

Play Charades.

Act out familiar titles of books, stories, and songs for a small group of classmates. Once a title has been guessed, write it on the board. Be sure to capitalize the words in the title correctly.

Teacher: Cut apart the activities and distribute to students based on the modalities that are their strengths.
(Visual) Have students cover each correct answer and correct the other title.
(Auditory) Students may use real titles or make up their own.
(Kinesthetic) If students are not familiar with how to play Charades, briefly explain the rules.

Reteach Activities • Titles and Quotation Marks

Hyphens

Underline words that should have hyphens. Write the hyphenated word on the line.

Our school is having an old fashioned carnival.   old-fashioned

Each carnival worker will wear a special T shirt.   T-shirt

I get to operate the merry go round.   merry-go-round

Mei will run tic tac toe games for the little children.   tic-tac-toe

Visual

Hyphens

Say phrases about carnivals to a partner. Include phrases with compound words that should be hyphenated and phrases with no hyphenated words. Have your partner listen and trace a hyphen in the air whenever a hyphen is needed. Then have your partner spell the hyphenated words. Take turns speaking and listening.

Auditory

Hyphens

Write the words below on index cards.

Write hyphens on index cards also. With a partner, arrange the words and hyphens so that the words are joined together correctly. Some words can be used in more than one combination.

| me | sister | law | twenty | one | green | five | old | time |
| fashioned | forget | not | blue | out | in | way |

Kinesthetic

Teacher: Cut apart the activities and distribute to students based on the modalities that are their strengths.
(Visual) Let pairs of students compare their underlined words before writing the hyphenated words on the lines.
(Auditory) Students may use the hyphenated words in the *Pupil Edition* as a resource.
(Kinesthetic) Suggest that students check their answers by looking up the hyphenated words in a dictionary.

66 Unit 6 • Chapter 32   Reteach Activities • Titles and Quotation Marks

Quotation Marks in Direct Quotations

Underline the words that are direct quotations. Add quotation marks.

"Watch this," the basketball player told her teammate.

The crowd yelled, "Do it again!"

"She's the best player on our team," explained the coach.

"She's the best I've ever seen," stated the reporter.

"We should win the game," the coach remarked.

Visual

Quotation Marks in Direct Quotations

What sport do you like the most?

Have a short conversation with a partner about a sport you enjoy playing or watching. Ask a third person to listen. Have that person repeat as much of the conversation as possible and use phrases like *he said* and *she said*. You and your partner can listen and snap your fingers whenever quotation marks are needed.

Auditory

Quotation Marks in Direct Quotations

Talk with a partner about your feelings about sports. Write each sentence on a sentence strip. Use phrases like *he said* or *she said* with each direct quotation. Check the sentences to make sure you used quotation marks in every sentence. Then mix up the strips and put them back in order to re-create your conversation.

Kinesthetic

Teacher: Cut apart the activities and distribute to students based on the modalities that are their strengths.
(Visual) Remind students that quotation marks always come in sets.
(Auditory) Pairs of students should make up short conversations of four or five sentences before switching roles.
(Kinesthetic) As students reread their conversations, have them circle the quotation marks.

Reteach Activities • More About Quotation Marks   Unit 6 • Chapter 34   67

Quotation Marks with Dialogue

Circle the correct sentence. Add quotation marks where they belong.

"I'm taking skating lessons now," said Eric.

"That's a good choice," replied Gillian. "You'll be able to play hockey or enter speed-skating races."

("I want to be a great speed-skater!" Eric exclaimed.)

Gillian answered, "You'd better start practicing now."

Visual

Quotation Marks with Dialogue

In a small group, brainstorm a list of words you could use in place of *said* **in a dialogue.** Post the list so that everyone can see it. Choose a word from the list, but keep it a secret. Then say a direct quotation in the way the word suggests. Have other group members listen and choose an appropriate word from the list to make up the statement that shows who was speaking. Have each group member take a turn speaking.

Auditory

Quotation Marks with Dialogue

Cut out the paragraph symbol. The symbol is a proofreading symbol that shows where to indent. With a partner, make up a skit about sports. Perform your skit before a small group of classmates. Have your classmates hold up their paragraph cards whenever a new speaker begins speaking.

Kinesthetic

Teacher: Cut apart the activities and distribute to students based on the modalities that are their strengths.
(Visual) Have students write the next line of dialogue. Remind them to indent for a new speaker.
(Auditory) Students can use the *Pupil Edition* or fiction books with dialogue to help them brainstorm ways to say dialogue.
(Kinesthetic) If students are unfamiliar with the paragraph symbol, demonstrate how to use it in proofreading written work.

68 Unit 6 • Chapter 34   Reteach Activities • More About Quotation Marks

Punctuating Dialogue

If a sentence is punctuated correctly, write *correct*. If it isn't, write *incorrect* on the line and add the necessary punctuation marks.

_____incorrect_____ "Now it's time to give out the sports awards," announced the principal.

_____incorrect_____ "Our first award goes to Megan," Coach Thomas said.

_____correct_____ Megan exclaimed, "I never expected to get an award!"

Visual

- ✂

Punctuating Dialogue

What is your favorite sport?

    Read aloud a few sentences of dialogue from a fiction book about sports. Read slowly so that your partner can listen and write the sentences. Work together to check the punctuation. Then switch roles.

Auditory

- ✂

Punctuating Dialogue

With a partner, role-play being sportscasters.

    Tell about part of an exciting game in a familiar sport. Tape-record your sportscast. Then play it back, and write it as a dialogue. Check your punctuation, and then give the written dialogue to another pair of students to read.

Kinesthetic

- ✂

Teacher: Cut apart the activities and distribute to students based on the modalities that are their strengths.
(Visual) Have volunteers write the sentences on the board so that students can check their work.
(Auditory) Suggest that students choose books for younger children to ensure shorter sentences and simpler sentence structure.
(Kinesthetic) If a tape recorder is not available, have other students record the dialogue as the actors say it.

Reteach Activities • More About Quotation Marks

Easily Confused Words: Homophones

Put a check above homophones that are correct. Cross out homophones that are wrong, and write the correct homophones above them.

Sallie ~~herd~~ [heard] that she could improve her health ~~buy~~ [by] eating better.

You ~~no~~ [know] you can eat better, too. ✓

~~Due~~ [Do] you know ✓ about the food pyramid?

Just tape it ~~too~~ [to] ~~you're~~ [your] refrigerator door.

Visual

Easily Confused Words: Homophones

What is nutrition?

Read aloud from a health and nutrition book. Have your partner listen and raise his or her hand when you say a homophone. Ask your partner to spell the homophone correctly. Check the spelling against the word in the book. Take turns reading and listening.

Auditory

Easily Confused Words: Homophones

Write the homophones below on separate index cards. Mix up the cards and lay them face down. With a partner, take turns choosing a card and making up a sentence that includes the homophone. If your sentence is correct, keep the card. Continue until all the cards are gone.

to/too/two	they're/their/there	its/it's	your/you're	know/no
knew/new	heard/herd	deer/dear	write/right	won/one	for/four

Kinesthetic

Teacher: Cut apart the activities and distribute to students based on the modalities that are their strengths.
(Visual) Have students use dictionaries to check their work.
(Auditory) Students might use their health or science textbooks or a library book.
(Kinesthetic) Have students review the meanings of the homophones in the *Pupil Edition* before beginning.

Negatives

Underline each negative in the paragraph.

I know that sweets are <u>not</u> as healthful as other foods. I try <u>not</u> to eat sweets very often. I just eat them when there is <u>no</u> fruit in the refrigerator. That <u>doesn't</u> usually happen around our house. I <u>can't</u> say that I <u>never</u> eat sweets though. <u>Nobody</u> can be a healthful eater all the time.

- Visual ✂

Negatives

What are some healthful foods?

Say aloud a sentence about healthful eating. Don't use negative words in your sentence. Have your partner listen and repeat your sentence. Then have your partner use a negative to give your sentence the opposite meaning.

- Auditory ✂

Negatives

Suppose that you and a partner are on a public television show about health and nutrition.

You are the interviewer, and your partner is a food expert. Ask your partner questions, and have him or her answer them. Whenever you or your partner says a negative word, shake your heads as you do when you want to say *no*.

- Kinesthetic ✂

Teacher: Cut apart the activities and distribute to students based on the modalities that are their strengths.
(Visual) Tell students there are seven negatives in the paragraph.
(Auditory) Have students explain how using a negative changes the meaning of the original sentence.
(Kinesthetic) Students might complete this activity in a small group.

Reteach Activities • Negatives and Easily Confused Words   Unit 6 • Chapter 35   71

Avoiding Double Negatives

Circle the sentence if it is correct. Change a word to correct an incorrect sentence.

Hank doesn't eat nothing but vegetables. *(anything)*

(Nancy won't ever eat french fries.)

Leroy never eats no vegetables. *(any)*

Harry won't eat french fries or salads neither. *(either)*

Visual

Avoiding Double Negatives

What is a healthful meal?

Describe a healthful meal to a partner. Use a double negative every few sentences. When your partner hears a double negative in a sentence, he or she should say "No!" and then say the sentence correctly.

Auditory

Avoiding Double Negatives

Think about the foods you eat.

On a sentence strip, write a sentence about them using a double negative. Give your sentence to a partner. Have your partner correct your sentence by cutting out one of the negative words.

Kinesthetic

Teacher: Cut apart the activities and distribute to students based on the modalities that are their strengths.
(Visual) Have students compare their answers to see whether some sentences have more than one correct answer.
(Auditory) As an alternative, have students draw a healthful meal on a paper plate and describe the meal to their partners.
(Kinesthetic) Students can use incorrect sentences from the *Pupil Edition* as models.

72 Unit 6 • Chapter 35   Reteach Activities • Negatives and Easily Confused Words

Skills Index

GRAMMAR

Adjectives, 43, 45, 47–48
Adverbs, 44–48
Nouns, 5–6, 13–14, 16–18
    subjects, 5–6
    more about nouns, 13–14
    possessive nouns, 16–18
Prepositions, 49–51
Pronouns, 37–42
Sentences, 1–3, 10–12, 52–60
    sentences, 1–3
    simple and compound sentences, 10–12
    phrases and clauses, 52–54
    complex sentences, 55–57
    sentence fragments and run–on sentences, 58–60
Verbs, 7–9, 19–36
    predicates, 7–9
    action verbs and linking verbs, 19–21
    main verbs and helping verbs, 22–23
    present–tense verbs, 25–27, 33
    past–tense verbs, 28–30, 33
    future–tense verbs, 31–33
    irregular verbs, 34–36

Skills Index

USAGE AND MECHANICS

Abbreviations, 15
Apostrophes, 16–18, 24
Be, 21
Combining Sentence Parts, 6, 9, 12
Colons, 62–63
Commas, 57, 61, 63
Contractions, 24
Easily Confused Words, 36, 42, 70
Exclamation Point, 2
Hyphens, 66
Negatives, 71–72
Periods, 1–3
Pronoun–Antecedent Agreement, 37
Question Marks, 1, 3
Quotation Marks, 67–69
Subject–Verb Agreement, 27, 30
Titles, 64–65